The Seventh Direction

A Legend of Creation

Kevin Locke

Kristy Cameron

Long ago, the world was created in seven days. Each day, **Wakȟáŋ Tȟáŋka** (The Great Spirit) began to create all of the mountains, trees, plants, animals, waters, and winds.

On the first four days, **Wakȟáŋ Tȟáŋka** stood facing the East, the South, the West and the North, and infused powers into each of those directions through his vision and words.

On the fifth day, **Wakȟáŋ Tȟáŋka** stood facing the Grandfather Sky and put all of the ancestors into motion, placing everything into perfect balance and symmetry.

On the sixth day, **Wakȟáŋ Tȟáŋka** stood facing the beautiful Grandmother Earth
and gifted her with the spirit of creation — the power of life and growth.

On the seventh day, **Wakȟáŋ Tȟáŋka** stood in the predawn darkness, facing the East. As the darkness began to give way to the light, the beauty of creation was born.

9

Suddenly, the first ray of light shot out from the horizon. It skimmed over the grasses and made them shimmer. It danced over the waters and made them sparkle. As it hit the trees, they burst into bloom.

The clouds were a beautiful pastel colour. The birds began to swoop, swirl, dart, and carol in the most beautiful way. With all of the animals moving around the Earth, at that precise moment, **Wakȟáŋ Tȟáŋka** realized it was now time to make the most precious and most sacred entity in the world — the human spirit.

At first, **Wakȟáŋ Tȟáŋka** was going to give the human spirit to the two-legged ones, but then thought: If I give it to them, will they fully realize how precious and sacred it is? If it is easy for them to get, they will undervalue it. But, if it is difficult to find, it will most certainly become precious to them.

All of the animals sensed an opportunity to offer a contribution. They all rushed forward, competing with each other to be the first to offer that perfect hiding place.

Tȟatȟáŋka (The Buffalo) said, "These vast prairies are my domain. I have the speed and the endurance to cross over them, and I can withstand bad weather. I shall take this precious human spirit and hide it. I will carry it far, where the prairies meet the mountains. I will hide it under the roots of a clump of buffalograss. They will never find it."

But, **Wakȟáŋ Tȟáŋka** said, "No, this will not do. In time, people will find this land and they will plow it with their large metal blades. All of the roots in the prairies will be made to stand upwards — there will be no hidden places. When they do this, the precious spirit will be discovered right away." **Tȟatȟáŋka** turned up his nose and went on his way.

Matȟó (The Bear) stepped up and said, "I'll hide it myself. I'll go beyond these prairies, way up into the mountains to my territory. I'll climb to the highest mountain and find the deepest cave to hide it. It will be safe there for all eternity. The two-legged will never find it."

But **Wakȟáŋ Tȟáŋka** shook his head and said, "No, no. These mountains, in time, will be filled with many people. They'll dig many holes and everything they see as valuable will be removed — there will be no hidden places. They'll find it right away." That **Matȟó**, he did not like this kind of rejection, and has been quite grouchy ever since.

One by one, each of the animals took turns offering a hiding place based on their own expertise. But, none of the ideas would work — none of them proved to be good enough.

The sun was beginning to set on the seventh day. They needed to hide the precious gift, otherwise it would not be part of the creation. That's when a little **Wahíŋheya** (Mole) popped up from underground. He held himself up in the last glimmers of light.

9

He said, "Wait, I know where we can hide it."

It is thought that the **Wahíŋheya** may be blind — that his eyes face inward toward his center.

"I can't see, but I have instinct. I sense that this creation is so beautiful that once the two-legged gaze upon it, they will be hypnotized by its beauty. They won't be able to rest until every part of it has been revealed."

"They'll be so thorough in their search, there won't be a blade of grass left unturned or a grain of sand left unsifted. But I know a place where it'll be safe. They will be so preoccupied looking everywhere else that this is the one place they'll never think to look."

This is where **Wakȟáŋ Tȟáŋka** placed the most sacred entity in all of creation: The human spirit. It is at the center of each of us. It is the place where all the powers of creation, all the powers of the four directions, Grandfather Sky, and Grandmother Earth are made to connect.

It is within our hearts.

The intersection of everything in this universe, this creation, is within each one of us. We have the responsibility to guard this precious gift as it does not belong to us but to **Wakȟáŋ Tȟáŋka**. We must do our best to be a good relative, not just to the two-leggeds, but to all of creation.

Lakota Language Words

The Great Spirit
Wakȟáŋ Tȟáŋka

Bear
Matȟó

East
Wiyóhiŋyaŋpata

Mole
Wahíŋheya

South
Itókataǧa

Buffalo
Tȟatȟáŋka

West
Wiyóȟpeyata

The Human Spirit
Taku Wakȟáŋ

North
Wazíyata

Grandfather Sky
Tȟuŋkášila Maȟpíya

Heart
Čhaŋté

Grandmother Earth
Uŋčí Makȟá

The Seven Directions

North
Wazíyata

South
Itókataǧa

East
Wiyóhiŋyaŋpata

West
Wiyóȟpeyata

Above
Grandfather Sky
Tȟuŋkášila Maȟpíya

Below
Grandmother Earth
Uŋčí Makȟá

Center
The Human Spirit
Taku Wakȟáŋ

Kevin Locke is a world-renowned Hoop Dancer, distinguished Indigenous Northern Plains flutist, traditional storyteller, cultural ambassador, recording artist, and educator. Kevin is Lakota (from the Hunkpapa Band of the Lakota Sioux), and Anishinabe. His Lakota name is Tȟokéya Inážiŋ, meaning "First to Arise." Kevin Locke presents and performs at hundreds of performing arts centers, festivals, schools, universities, conferences, state and national parks, monuments, historic sites, powwows, and reservations every year. Approximately eighty percent of these are shared with children. Kevin is a dance and musical hero and role model for youth around the world. His special joy is working with children on reservations to ensure the survival and growth of Indigenous culture.

www.kevinlocke.com
www.patricialockefoundation.org

Kristy Cameron, is a teacher, and artist who was born and raised in northwestern Ontario. Growing-up surrounded by the beauty of the natural world has given her endless subjects to paint. Kristy is a well-known artist who has collaborated in the past with writer David Bouchard, providing beautiful illustrations for his books including Seven Sacred Teachings. Kristy is of Métis descent and still lives in her hometown of Atikokan, Ontario Canada.

www.kristycameron.ca

Medicine Wheel Publishing

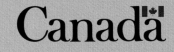

Funded by the
Government
of Canada

Financé par le
gouvernement
du Canada

Canada

ISBN: 978-1-77854-013-4
For more book information go to https://medicinewheelpublishing.com
Printed in PRC
Published in Canada by Medicine Wheel Publishing
Lakota language words and spelling referenced from the New Lakota Dictionary.